Popular Tree Frogs

By Philippe de Vosjoli,
Robert Mailloux &
Drew Ready

i-5
PRESS

All photos by Philippe de Vosjoli except where otherwise indicated
Cover photography by David Northcott.
The photographs in this book are courtesy of: Zig Leszczynski, p.8;
Paul Freed, pp. 19, 51; Bill Love, pg. 38; David Northcott, courtesy of
Nature's Lens, pp. 55, 57, 58, 59; Michael Ready, pp 31, 35; D.B.
Travis, pp. 7, 27, 37, 39, 49, 53, 56, 71.

i-5 PUBLISHING, LLC™
Chief Executive Officer: Mark Harris
Chief Financial Officer: Nicole Fabian
Vice President, Chief Content Officer: June Kikuchi
General Manager, i-5 Press: Christopher Reggio
Art Director, i-5 Press: Mary Ann Kahn
Vice President, General Manager Digital: Jennifer Black
Production Director: Laurie Panaggio
Production Manager: Jessica Jaensch
Marketing Director: Lisa MacDonald

Original Print ISBN 978-1-882770-77-9

i-5 Publishing, LLC™
3 Burroughs, Irvine, CA 92618
www.facebook.com/i5press
www.i5publishing.com

CONTENTS

INTRODUCTION

Recently, United States herpetoculturists have focused on a more naturalistic approach to keeping reptiles and amphibians. Many keepers now house their animals in naturalistic vivaria—captive environments that simulate certain essential characteristics of an animal's natural habitat—a trend that has led to increased interest in the small animals that thrive in these new kinds of enclosures.

Among the best vivarium animals are tree frogs, stunning creatures that perch on virtually anything—including glass walls, branches, and leaves—and make for incredible display animals. Certain species of these frogs even can be kept with other small frogs and lizards in a community vivarium, allowing keepers to create vibrant habitats in their own home. Unfortunately, just as the interest in tropical amphibians is increasing, availability appears to be diminishing, the result of lack of knowledge, lack of standards for commercial exploitation, protective legislation (some of which is unsound), habitat destruction, and environmental and climatic changes. If people are to enjoy frogs and other amphibians in the future, sound conservation, research, and management of various species must receive immediate attention, and herpetologists must establish self-sustainable populations of as many species as possible.

The authors' original goal was to write a simple, basic book on the care of popular tree frogs, but during the writing process it became obvious that successful frog keeping requires certain skills and knowledge—much like keeping tropical fish. Although there are a number of books about the care of amphibians, several were written by authors with little or no experience in keeping or breeding frogs, and few contain any valuable information.

This book, written by experienced and recognized frog herpetoculturists, focuses on the care of popular tree frogs now sold in pet stores. It covers many important topics, from acclimating imported species to housing, feeding, and captive-breeding. It is a practical manual for the serious hobbyist who cares about the welfare of his or her animals.

CHAPTER 1

GENERAL INFORMATION AND SELECTION

What are Tree Frogs?

Tree frog is the popular term for arboreal and semi-arboreal, nocturnal frogs that have toe pads at the ends of their digits. The common name "tree frog" is usually reserved for members of the family Hylidae, but the popular herpetocultural definition also includes the glass frogs (family Centronelidae), reed frogs (family Hyperolidae), and flying frogs (family Rhacophoridae).

Selecting Tree Frogs

If you are new to keeping tree frogs, your best bet is to begin with a species that has simple, clear-cut care requirements; possibilities include White's tree frogs (*Litoria caerulea*), white-lipped tree frogs (*L. infrafrenata*), green tree frogs (*Hyla cinerea*), and Cuban tree frogs (*Osteopiius septentrionalis*). Other tree frogs require some experience, particularly if they are wild-caught imports, but, if you follow the instructions in this book, you also should have success with moderately difficult-to-keep species, such as the ever-popular red-eyed tree frogs.

As a rule, species that require cool, temperate conditions, or hail from a cloud forest or tropical rainforest tend to be more difficult to keep than the more adaptable temperate and subtropical species. This is usually because cloud-forest and rainforest species have specific habitat requirements—such as a particular landscape, temperate range, relative humidity range, or air flow—that need to be duplicated if the frogs are to survive for a long time.

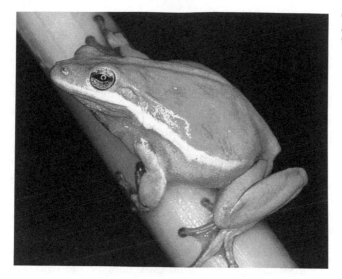

However, researching the habitat and niche of particular
tree frogs, acquiring experience at establishing frogs, and
setting up the right type of vivaria will allow you to successfully keep and breed these more difficult species.

This book focuses on the care of easy-to-keep and
readily available species, but also includes information on
gliding tree frogs, an appealing species that has more
complex care requirements.

The first step to keeping tree frogs successfully is to select
the species that you can comfortably accommodate. The
second step is to select potentially healthy animals (see below).

Captive-Bred Versus Wild-Caught Specimens

White's tree frogs are captive-bred in large numbers in
the United States and are generally easy to rear to adult-
hood. Other captive-bred species are available less
frequently and, due to the small size and special requirements of their young, are often more difficult to rear.
Wild-caught adults of the popular species mentioned in
this book (with the exception of gliding tree frogs) are
relatively easy to establish in captivity and are probably as
good a choice as captive-bred frogs. However, keeping
more difficult species, whether wild-caught or captive-

bred, will prove challenging, and very possibly disappointing, to inexperienced herpetoculturists.

Selecting Healthy Tree Frogs

To have success with tree frogs, you must select healthy specimens. The following guidelines will help you make the right choice:

1. Select species that you can accommodate. Research the needs and vivarium design requirements of whatever species you plan to purchase, and make sure you have the time, money, and space to meet their requirements. Your frogs will not survive unless you provide them with the proper captive conditions.

2. Observe the animals you plan to purchase. Generally, tree frogs that perch on the glass sides or the landscape structures of a vivarium prove healthier than those that remain on the ground. However, this is only a guideline, not an absolute rule. Occasionally, if a store owner or seller keeps their frogs in the wrong kind of vivarium, stressed tree frogs may seek terrestrial shelters or specimens may move to the ground to reduce dehydration or find cooler temperatures.

3. Carefully inspect the animal. It should not have sores, lumps, swollen legs, or clouded eyes. Its body should appear rounded, and the outlines of its hip bones, backbone, and skull should not be prominent.

A healthy White's tree frog has very smooth rounded contours.

4. When held in your hand, the frog should demonstrate definite signs of vigor. A frog that seems limp or weak is usually very ill. Once you have a frog in hand, reinspect its body, including its ventral area (underside), for sores or redness. Avoid animals that have these symptoms.
5. If the frogs are kept on paper substrate, look for signs of feces. Watery, runny feces usually indicate illness, and bloody feces are a definite sign of physical problems.

If the frog you select has met these criteria, there is a good chance that it is relatively healthy and will acclimate to captivity, given the proper conditions.

Aerosols and Miticides

Aerosol sprays, such as hair spray, perfume deodorants, and disinfectants, can kill tree frogs. The frogs absorb the aerosols through their skin and, thereafter, often suffer painful deaths. Do not keep frogs in areas (e.g., bathrooms or kitchens) where aerosols are used. High concentrations of or long-term exposure to No Pest strips, used for killing mites, will also kill frogs.

CHAPTER 2

ACCLIMATION AND HOUSING

Acclimation

The first few weeks of keeping a new tree frog are among the most difficult. Specimens may harbor parasites, suffer from illnesses, or have difficulty adjusting to their new surroundings. In order to ensure the animal's survival, keepers should adhere to the guidelines presented below. Use the following steps to establish imported or wild-caught tree frogs in captivity:

1. Keep newly acquired frogs in a room with a cool-air humidifier (available at most drug stores), which will keep the relative humidity between 60 and 70 percent. Humidifiers are not necessary in regions with moderate to high relative humidity. Do not keep frogs at saturated humidity levels (above 85 percent).

2. To create a tree frog vivarium, place your frog in a large plastic terrarium or glass vivarium, supplying white paper towel as substrate and a shallow water bowl or saucer as a water source. With baby frogs, add a shallow container filled with moist moss. Lean a piece of bark against one side of the terrarium in order to provide a vertical shelter and place another on the ground as a ground-level shelter. Keep the vivarium at the temperature range appropriate for the species. Provide moderately bright light with overhead, full-spectrum fluorescent bulbs for twelve hours a day.

3. If the frog appears weak, has sores on its snout or body, or has clouded eyes, monitor it for a few days to see if it improves. If it does not, treat it with injectable

enrofloxacin (Baytril), subcutaneously in the ventral area, at a dosage of 10 milligrams per kilogram (mg/kg) of the frog's body weight. Repeat the treatment every two days for up to two weeks.

4. Monitor the stools of your frog during its acclimation period. Healthy frogs have soft, well-formed stools. Watery and runny feces are signs of parasites or gastrointestinal disease.

5. Offer crickets of the appropriate size to your tree frog every two to three days, and monitor the status of its feces. If the feces are runny, treat the frog orally with metronidazole (Flagyl) at 50 mg/kg of the frog's total body weight. Repeat the treatment in one week. Using metronidazole twice, at seven-day intervals, during enrofloxacin treatment can be beneficial because of its beneficial antibiotic effects on anaerobic bacteria. If your tree frog has nematodes in its stools, treat it with fenbendazole (Panacur) at 50 mg/kg, and repeat the process once or twice at seven-day intervals. To orally administer drugs or water, use a wedge cut from a plastic deli cup or yogurt container, and insert it gently between the frog's jaws. For larger species or specimens, gently place an inverted spoon between the animal's jaws to keep its mouth open.

6. If a frog refuses to feed, open its mouth and insert a prekilled cricket of the appropriate size. In most cases,

Although adult tree frogs can be kept for extended periods in a basic setup like this temporary quarantine vivarium, it does not provide the proper conditions for a good quality of life. Experts recommend larger vivaria with plants and climbing areas.

tree frogs will swallow the cricket when released. If your frog is emaciated and not feeding on its own, use this feeding method as soon as possible.

7. If your newly imported frogs are sick or dehydrated, give them water orally in addition to providing a water bowl. Keep the water bowl clean and replace the water several times each week and whenever it is fouled. Lightly mist the frogs every evening.

8. Replace the paper towel substrate whenever it is fouled, and keep all water clean. Feed your frogs every two to three days, and monitor them closely. Healthy frogs are active at night, eat regularly, have formed feces, and eventually put on weight. Transfer your frog to a larger vivarium as soon as it shows signs that it has acclimated to captivity.

> **Warning!**
>
> Quarantine your frog for at least sixty days before introducing it to an established collection.

A Basic Vivarium

To create a basic tree frog vivarium suitable for quarantine or maintenance, you first need an all-glass enclosure with a screen top. For most species, experts recommend at least a 20-gallon tank. Tree frogs are active, and smaller enclosures

When quarantining red-eyed tree frogs, add potted plants or those grown hydroponically in jars to the enclosure. Chinese evergreen and pothos are the best choices.

do not provide the conditions they need to have a good quality of life. You can use smaller vivaria for quarantine and for rearing froglets.

When using at least a 20-gallon vivarium, keep most species at a ratio of one frog per 5 gallons (meaning you could house four frogs in a 20-gallon tank). With very large species, such as White's tree frogs or white-lipped tree frogs, experts recommend at least a 29-gallon vivarium and a frog-to-volume ratio of one frog per 15 gallons of vivarium space.

If you want a different look, put the sliding screen-top vivarium on its side to create a vertical vivarium. Ideally, use silicone to attach a section of acrylic or glass across the base, thereby making a bottom that will hold substrate and water without letting it seep out or clog the screen.

In a simply designed vivarium, newsprint or white paper towel substrate works with many species during quarantine, but it is not suitable for species that require high relative humidity unless they are kept in a room with a cool-air humidifier. The alternative is to use a 1- to 2-inch layer of smooth medium-grade pea gravel as a substrate. Make sure the pea gravel is large enough that your frogs cannot accidentally swallow it. If you add water up to half the substrate height, the surface of the substrate will remain dry, but the bottom will contain enough water to raise relative humidity. Provide water in a shallow container, such as a dog's water bowl or a plastic storage box (shoebox size). Make sure the water level in the container is no higher than that of the height of the frogs at rest.

Landscaping a Simple Vivarium

Place live plants, such as pothos ivy or Chinese evergreen, in jars of water or in gravel and water. They will serve as resting sites for your frogs and will help raise the relative humidity in the vivarium. If the air temperature is cool, place a red 25-watt (or higher) incandescent light bulb over a basking site. Use full-spectrum fluorescent lighting as the vivarium's primary source of light; it will benefit the frogs and the plants. You can raise relative humidity by simply increasing the number of plants in jars.

Baby tree frogs are prone to dehydration. Most species fare best in a gravel bed type of vivarium. For quarantine or other simple setups, create an area of moistened green moss and add a shallow water container. To prevent drowning, place a rock or strands of pothos vine in the water container.

Flush System Using a Pebble Substrate

A flush system works best with large vivaria—use at least a 30-gallon, all-glass tank, preferably something larger. To construct this type of enclosure, first place a 2- to 4-inch thick layer of medium-grade smooth pea gravel on the bottom of the tank. At one end, push back the gravel to create a pool area, essentially exposing the glass bottom of the enclosure. You can add rock or freshwater driftwood on the surface of the gravel. Use plants that can grow hydroponically (see page 16) as bare-root plants in the gravel bed. Place additional flora in pots, with only part of the pot buried.

Next, soak green sheet-moss in a bucket of water and place it over the gravel, covering the base of the plants but leaving the edges of the pool and the pool itself clear of the moss. Place smooth, round rocks along the edges of the pool to prevent gravel from sliding in, and for aesthetic purposes as well. Then add up to 2 inches of water to the enclosure. The pool will fill up, but the gravel surface will remain dry. You also can add a miniature waterfall to this system by placing the outflow tube above the water surface in whatever manner is most aesthetically pleasing.

Gravel bed vivaria are advantageous when keeping animals and plant species that require high relative humidity. To maintain the tank, mist the plants each day. Once a week, pour water over the substrate to flush wastes into the pool area, then remove the fouled water with a wet/dry vacuum cleaner. Wipe the bottom of the water section with paper towels to remove algae and slime that accumulated on its surface. Add fresh water to the water section, but not over the substrate. The plants growing hydroponically help remove ammonia from the water, as does the algae growing on rocks and other surfaces. If the gravel layer is deep, add soil over one section of it and introduce plants directly in the soil. To make this system more effective, add a small water pump that moves water from the pool area through the gravel substrate; the water flow allows the gravel to act as a biological filtering system.

Healthy frogs experience minimal problems with this system, and weekly flushing prevents the buildup of bacteria.

Orchid Bark

You can use fir-bark based orchid bark—not cedar bark—as a substrate for tree frogs. Keep the bark dry. If orchid bark remains wet for prolonged periods of time, it may leach out potentially harmful compounds.

Filtered Flush Systems

More elaborate flush systems pump water into the pool section through a filter. There are two ways to create such a system: one is to move the water over the gravel substrate as indicated previously. The other is to pump the water through a box containing a filtering medium. Pool filters work in large vivaria, but you can construct simple box filters from food storage containers by drilling a hole in two opposite sides of a container and filling it with carbon and filter floss or filter pads.

Naturalistic Vivarium

Among European herpetoculturists, naturalistic vivaria are one of the most popular systems for keeping frogs. First,

place a 1- to 2-inch layer of pea gravel on the bottom of a large, all-glass enclosure. Above the pea gravel, add a 2- or 3-inch layer of moistened, high-quality, peat moss-based potting soil. Plant various tropical plants directly in the growing medium. Appropriate selections include pothos ivy, Chinese evergreen, calatheas, philodendron, alocasia, and bromeliads that don't have spiny edges, such as neurogelias. Add landscape structures, such as rock, wood, or cork, to the setup. Bury a water container in the soil and add water to the container. Twice a week, remove the water container, wash it thoroughly, and replace the water. Disinfect the container in a 5 percent bleach solution once a month, then rinse it and allow it to soak in water with a dechlorinator for at least an hour before placing it back in the vivarium.

Alternatively, you can create a permanent, filtered water section. To do this, attach 2- to 3-inch tall glass walls to the sides and bottom of your vivarium with silicone sealant, creating an enclosed area. Add a small water pump that sends the water through a filter canister or through a sponge filter. You can also use an undergravel filter, but this requires adding a 1- to 2-inch layer of pea gravel on top of the filter plates. The drawback of fixed-water sections is that they need regular cleaning and water changes in order to prevent them from becoming vectors for disease. It is also necessary to clean or replace all filters on a regular basis.

Step-by-Step Naturalistic Vivarium Design

Many tree frogs do well in gravel bed vivaria. To create a gravel bed shallow shoreline vivarium, first add a 2- to 3-inch layer of washed pea gravel or larger grade aquarium gravel. In one corner, push the gravel aside to create a water area and line its edge with large, smooth stones to prevent gravel from sliding in. Add plants to the setup; choose types that can grow hydroponically and rinse them free of soil before putting them in the enclosure. Dig a hollow in the gravel, insert the plant and place gravel around its roots to anchor it in place. For tree frog vivaria, the best choice is Chinese evergreen (*Aglaonema*), but other possibilities include pothos (*Epipremnum*), arrowhead plants (*Syngonium*) and philodendron. Other plants, such as bromeliads and calathea, can be placed in pots on top of the gravel bed.

Add cork bark and freshwater driftwood as shelters and climbing areas. Place a layer of moistened green moss above large sections of the gravel substrate. This system works well with most *Hyla* species, such as green tree frogs, gray tree frogs, Pacific tree frogs, Chinese jade tree frogs, and a wide range of tropical forest and rain forest tree frogs (including red-eyed tree frogs). To maintain the setup, pour water over the moss area once a week to flush out wastes, then siphon or vacuum water from the water area once a week, and replace it with clean water added directly to the same area (not poured over the moss).

CHAPTER 3

TEMPERATURE AND HUMIDITY

Heating

Most tree frogs do not bask in sunlight like other reptiles, although several species appear to enjoy basking, usually in the later part of the day. Because of this, basking lights are not a good way to heat tree frog enclosures. In general, frogs should be kept in rooms that are in the range of their temperature tolerance. Room temperatures in the mid 70s °F are suitable for most tree frogs, although certain montane and cool-climate species require colder temperatures. Once the temperature in the room is in the general range of your tree frogs' requirements, you can provide supplemental heat by using subtank heating strips controlled by a rheostat, similar to electronic light dimmers, or thermostat, or by placing submersible heaters in the water

Two color variations of the barking tree frog.

section adjusted to keep the water in the correct temperature range. Some herpetoculturists place submersible heaters in large jars of water or put 25-watt red incandescent bulbs over select areas. If controlled by a rheostat or pulse-proportional thermostat, low-wattage infrared ceramic bulbs also work in large enclosures. In the authors' opinion, the best choice is to keep your frogs in a room that is heated to their temperature requirements and not to supply additional heating.

Cooling

Few tree frogs currently collected or imported for the pet trade require unusually cool temperatures. If you decide to keep cool-temperature or montane species, use a thermostat-controlled air conditioner to keep the room cool. During emergencies or heat waves, place jars of ice in the vivarium and cover it with Styrofoam to prevent it from overheating. In dry climates, "swamp coolers" (evaporative coolers) may be adequate for lowering room temperature to a satisfactory level.

Relative Humidity

Proper relative humidity is critical to the successful maintenance and breeding of frogs. Most frogs thrive in 60 to 70 percent moderate relative humidity (use a hygrometer to measure relative humidity). This level is easily maintained in naturalistic vivaria or vivaria with hydroponic plants. If necessary, use a cool-air humidifier to raise the relative humidity of a room. Lightly misting a vivarium one or more times each day will also increase relative humidity. In an unventilated area, saturated humidity levels are fatal to most tree frogs; never keep tree frogs in glass covered vivaria.

You can condition many tropical tree frogs for breeding by keeping them at a lower relative humidity for a few weeks or months, thereby simulating a dry season. During this conditioning, do not mist the enclosure, to keep the frogs drier, but leave a water container as the primary source of moisture.

CHAPTER 4

DIET AND WATER

Diet

All tree frogs are primarily insectivorous, although large specimens occasionally ingest vertebrate prey. The easiest approach to feeding tree frogs is to offer them commercially raised insects. Use the following guidelines when feeding your frogs:

Gray Crickets (*Acheta domestica*)

Gray crickets should be a primary component of the diet of captive tree frogs. Most stores that sell amphibians and reptiles also sell these crickets in a variety of sizes suitable for feeding a wide range of tree frogs, from newly metamorphosed froglets to much larger species. Feeder crickets should be about the same length as the head of the tree frog. This general rule works with other kinds of food items also, even mice. Before offering the insects to your tree frogs, house them in a small plastic terrarium for twenty-four hours and feed them a high-quality diet (see page 23).

Flies

You can purchase housefly maggots through mail order companies and keep them in jars or screened enclosures until they pupate and metamorphose. Using houseflies is a cheap way to feed large numbers of froglets and provide a good supplemental food for adult tree frogs. They are best used in greenhouse facilities, where escaped flies will not be as much of an annoyance as in your home. However, if you allow them to pupate in jars, you can funnel them into a vivarium with a nylon stocking; cut off the toe-end of the stocking, attach it to the pupating jar, and guide the flies from the jar into the frog vivaria.

Fruit Flies

The large flightless fruit fly (*Drosophila hydei)* is a good supplemental dietary item for froglets (check *Reptiles* and *Reptiles USA* for mail order sources). These flies are easy to raise using a standard fruit fly mix, which is available by mail order or through biological supply houses.

Mealworms and Superworms

Mealworms (*Tenebrio molitor*) and superworms (*Zophobas molitor*) should be offered to tree frogs only as part of a varied diet. White mealworms (recently molted) are more easily digested and are preferable as a diet to chitinized ones. Larger tree frog species fare better than smaller species on diets that include mealworms, particularly superworms.

Wax Worms (*Galleria mellonella*)

Normally, you should offer wax moth caterpillars to your frogs, although many tree frogs relish metamorphosed moths. Wax moths also make good food for imported tree frogs that are reluctant to feed; often, they provide incentive for the reluctant feeder to start eating.

Mice

Sparingly feed baby (pink) mice and preweaned mice to larger tree frogs. Most experts believe that a mice-heavy diet is not good for the long-term health of tree frogs. Large frogs often become grotesquely obese on this diet. This condition may appeal to some frog keepers but, as in humans, fatty and rich diets are not healthy for tree frogs and can lead to a number of diseases. An acceptable basic tree frog diet consists of one mouse once or twice a month, combined with foods lower in fat and protein (including insects that have been fed vegetable matter). It is very likely that, in the wild, large frogs occasionally ingest other vertebrates, though these vertebrates are probably smaller frogs, not mice.

Frogs

Some tree frogs feed on other frogs. Indeed, for some species, such as members of the genus *Hemiphractus*, other frogs constitute a significant component of the diet. Unless you work with frog-eating species, it is best to feed your tree frogs a non-frog diet. When feeding your tree frogs other frogs (especially those collected in the wild), you run the risk of exposing your animals to parasites and diseases.

Feeding Commercially Raised Insects

Most experts believe that it is important to feed feeder insects a high-quality diet and that doing so is key to the proper maintenance of tree frogs. Because of their opportunistic feeding habits, gray crickets are easy to "gut-load" with a variety of high quality foods. Gut-loading is the process of feeding feeder insects a high-quality diet with select vitamins and minerals. Once your insects have fed on this high-quality diet, "loading" their guts with nutritious vitamins and minerals, offer them to your animals.

To do this, place crickets in a plastic terrarium twenty-four hours before feeding them to your frogs and offer them calcium-rich greens such as kale, collards, or mustard greens; finely chopped vegetables such as grated squashes, carrots, and mixed vegetables; and occasional fruit. Sprinkle a small amount of powdered calcium carbonate on the food before

Every time a frog eats, it ingests the gut contents of the insects it captures. Feeding crickets a high-quality diet (several are now on the market) along with slices of carrot or oranges will optimize their nutritional value.

offering it to the insects. Every third feeding, feed the crickets a commercial cricket diet, powdered ground rodent chow, or food-processed grains, such as oatmeal, barley, or sesame seed (in small amounts) mixed with calcium carbonate. In the long run, an excessively fatty or rich diet will have a negative effect on amphibians and reptiles, so you should not feed crickets with an exclusively commercial cricket diet, even though it is convenient.

Vitamin and Mineral Supplementation

For adult frogs, many keepers supplement feeder insects once a week using a mix consisting of one-half calcium carbonate or calcium gluconate and one-half powdered multivitamin/mineral supplement, such as Reptivite or Herptivite. For approximately every cupful of this mix, add two human vitamin B-complex tablets, finely pulverized with a mortar and pestle; additional B vitamins may be beneficial in helping frogs fight certain pathogens.

Before feeding, place a small amount of the mix in a jar with the feeder insects and gently stir the jar, lightly coating the insects. The key word here is lightly—you do not want so much mix that the crickets are white or beige with supplementation. They should appear lightly dusted. Because juveniles and immature frogs undergo rapid growth, supplement their diet twice a week.

Metabolic Bone Disease and Vitamin D$_3$

Like lizards, tree frogs fed a calcium- and vitamin-deficient diet will develop metabolic bone disease. In frogs, the first symptom is usually an inability to feed. By that time, the frog's jaw bones have become soft and flexible. Other symptoms include backbone deformities, splayed hind legs (the result of soft hip bones) and, in time, soft limbs. The lower jaw of an afflicted specimen may even droop or grow beyond the end of the upper jaw. If the disease has not progressed too far, liquid calcium and vitamins, which can be hand-fed with a feeding syringe, generally reverses the effects.

To assist-feed a tree frog, place pre-killed crickets in its mouth or use a syringe filled with Emeraid 2 (made by

Lafeber's) or Exact bird hand-feeding formula (made by Kaytee). Administer the formula directly into the stomach, not in the mouth; frogs are built to swallow whole prey. When force feeding a large frog, gently insert a tuberculin syringe (containing feeding formula) past its throat and into its stomach. In smaller species, you can gain access to the stomach by connecting line tubing (such as model airplane fuel line tubing) to the end of a syringe filled with a liquefied diet. This procedure requires experience, however, and is best left to the more specialized keeper.

Though research is currently underway, studies have yet to show whether vitamin D_3 is significant in tree frogs' ability to absorb calcium. There is little doubt that some tree frogs bask some of the time, usually toward dusk. For those species, at least, exposure to ultraviolet (UV) rays may play a role in their synthesis of vitamin D_3. On the other hand, many species seldom or never expose themselves to sunlight, and this eliminates the significance of UV rays for D_3 synthesis in these frogs. In such cases, if vitamin D_3 is significant in calcium absorption, it must have a dietary source.

Currently, the standard procedure is to lightly supplement the diet of tree frogs by feeding them crickets coated with a powdered commercial reptile vitamin/mineral supplement, and many herpetoculturists also provide full-spectrum lighting for their tree frogs. For larger tree frogs, you can occasionally offer whole prey, such as pink or fuzzy mice, as a source of vitamin D_3, but the mice should make up only a small portion of a tree frog's diet.

Hypervitaminosis

Hypervitaminosis in captive frogs has seldom been reported, partially because herpetoculturists usually do not associate a frog's symptoms with hypervitaminosis. If tree frogs are fed high levels of vitamin D_3 and calcium, they may suffer kidney damage, which results in water edema of the limbs and body. Experts suspect that other symptoms— such as calcium deposits in the internal organs, signs of metabolic bone disease, and other symptoms similar to those found in reptiles—also occur in oversupplemented frogs. To avoid hypervitaminosis, feed your insects a high-quality diet that includes natural foods, such as greens, vegetables, fruit, and a small percentage of grains and processed foods. In addition, remember to lightly supplement your food insects.

Water

Tree frogs need clean water at all times. Offer it in a shallow water container, such as a plastic storage box or a pet bowl, or through a water section designed specifically for your vivarium. Change the water at least twice each week and whenever it is fouled with fecal matter. Wash the container once every week or two with an antibacterial dish detergent, then thoroughly rinse the container before refilling it with

Unless you have high-quality tap water, use bottled or carbon-filtered water in your frogs' vivarium. Allow tap water to sit so that the harmful gases and chlorine dissipate.

water. Use high-quality water, such as bottled drinking water or carbon-filtered water. Make sure the water is also chlorine free; simply let it sit for twenty-four hours, and most of the chlorine will dissipate.

An Albino Pacific tree frog. This morph will soon be available commercially.

CHAPTER 5

CAPTIVE BREEDING

From a herpetological or economic standpoint, few common tree frogs are worth breeding. For these species, it is smarter to collect tadpoles on a regular basis and raise them indoors until they metamorphose into froglets. Greenhouse or screenhouse herpetoculture, which can be accomplished where these frogs naturally occur, is an excellent approach to captive propagation of common species, but proper management of wild tree frog populations may be a more viable financial option than indoor captive-breeding.

The opposite is the case with more uncommon tree frogs. Any serious frog herpetoculturist knows that rare or unusual frogs are seldom available and that every effort should be made to establish them in herpetoculture, in case they become completely unavailable. Phyllomedusine tree frogs, any colorful tropical hylids (such as *Hyla leucophyllata*), the gliding tree frogs of the genus *Rhacophorus*, and the crowned tree frog *Anotheca spinosa* are all among the most desired species.

To begin any breeding project, first make sure:
1. You have one (preferably several) healthy adult pair.
2. The breeding pairs have good weight, but are not obese. Good muscle tone, common in tree frogs raised in large enclosures that allow them to be active, is also desirable.

Rain Chambers

Rain chambers are extremely effective tools for encouraging various frog species to breed in captivity. They are particularly effective after the frogs get a winter rest—for tropical species this rest should be under cooler conditions that involve a period of lower relative humidity and drier conditions. Members of the genus *Litoria*, for example, breed readily after proper conditioning (cooler and drier) followed by exposure to rain chamber conditions. Rain chambers are also effective with recently imported tree frogs, likely because they have been collected at the onset of their breeding season. If your recent imports are healthy and appear to be in breeding condition (signified by nuptial pads in males and bulging abdomens in females), introduce them into the breeding chamber—you may have immediate success.

Building a Rain Chamber

To create a rain chamber, begin with a 40- or 55-gallon aquarium with a screen top, and place a water pump on the bottom of the tank. Link the pump to PVC pipe and run the pipe up one side of the aquarium and along the length of the top or inner back side. Plant sprinkler heads in the PVC pipe every 6 to 8 inches or drill multiple holes in the pipe. Add water to a depth of 3 to 6 inches, depending on the size of the species. Place floating sections of Styrofoam on almost one-quarter of the water surface, and add some plants, such as water hyacinth or hydroponically grown arrowhead plants. If you use enough plants, Styrofoam sections are not necessary.

Another method for creating a rain chamber is to run a small water pump into a container with a finely perforated bottom and rest the container on top of a screen-topped

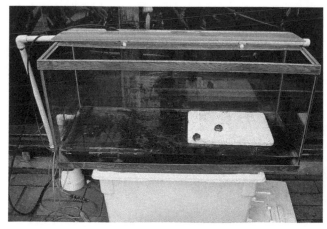

A simple rain chamber using an aquarium with a glass cover, a submersible water pump, a PVC pipe adaptor, PVC pipe, and irrigation system sprinkler heads. For a simple and effective alternative to sprinkler heads, drill small holes along the length of the horizontal PVC sprinkler bar.

glass enclosure. With this type of system, make sure that the rate of outflow is equal to the rate of inflow, or the storage container may overfill and cause flooding. Set the pumps with standard timers or timers that allow for multiple settings.

Misting

Extensive misting, done manually or automatically several times each evening, can induce breeding in several types of frogs. Many tropical frog species that lay eggs in foam nests or egg masses on plants above a water area (like many of the Phyllomedusine tree frogs) will breed after a prebreeding conditioning period of three to eight weeks, during which they are kept drier, with no misting, and provided with only a dish of standing water for their water source. After this conditioning, return them to a standard maintenance schedule that also includes daily misting for twenty to thirty minutes three times a day, or exposure to a rain chamber for two to four hours daily. Phyllomedusine frogs, including the popular red-eyed tree frog (*Agalychnis callidryas*) breed readily under this system, as do many other tropical forest frogs, including foam nest-building rhaeophorids and various small tropical hylids, such as the hourglass frog (*H. ebraccata*).

Additional Breeding Stimuli

Many frog species are sexually stimulated by the croaking

A pair of White's tree frogs in amplexus.

This red-eyed tree frog egg mass shows developing embryos.

(and other sounds) of male frogs of their own species. Anyone who has come upon breeding groups of frogs has heard dozens, or even hundreds, of male frogs chorusing. Unfortunately, herpetoculturists are usually able to obtain only a few specimens of a particular species. Playing back recorded sound of males croaking provides additional stimulation for captive specimens to breed.

Breeding

None of the tree frogs mentioned in this book are particularly difficult to breed, and the following factors should lead to successful breeding:

1. Breeding probability is increased when you keep several pairs of frogs together, at least during the breeding season.
2. As mentioned, frogs that are conditioned for breeding should be healthy and have good weight but should not be grossly obese.
3. Experts recommend winter cooling of four to ten weeks, while keeping the frogs at a lower relative humidity, prior to breeding.
4. Time cooling so that the frogs are exposed to real or simulated rain during low-pressure barometric conditions, such as when a real storm is in your area. This increases the probability of breeding.

5. Provide large enclosures with large water areas. Frog spawns tend to be large, and if the frogs breed in a small water area, there is a high risk that eggs or tadpoles will die because of reduced oxygen in the water. It is also dangerous to add water later because all tank water must sit and dechlorinate for several days.

Standard Breeding Procedure

When considering breeding tree frogs, first research their natural history and the climatic patterns of their native environment. After you have conducted your research, use the following rough guidelines:

1. **Temperate tree frogs:** Keep temperate species cooler and drier (no misting) for one to two months during the winter. Study the climatic tolerance of your species to determine the proper winter temperature levels for the vivarium. Usually, temperatures ranging in the 60s °F during the day and the 50s °F at night are adequate for most temperate species. During the cooling period, keep the vivarium's photoperiod at ten hours of light every twenty-four hours.

   After the cooling period, feed the frogs well for two to three weeks, then place pairs in a rain chamber, setting the timer for the water pump to run from 6 PM to 10 PM. Keep this regimen for several days, and breeding will usually occur within a week if your frogs are ready to breed. Remember that many species may breed a second, and even a third, time if they have been fed well for at least three weeks before their exposure to a rain chamber.

2. **Tropical tree frogs:** As a general rule, many tropical species of tree frogs will breed if kept at a lower relative humidity (no misting) and slightly cooler (5–8 °F) for one to two months, then fed well for a couple of weeks and exposed to daily misting or rain chamber conditions for several hours. Mist frogs and place them in rain chambers in the early evening—for up to five days with species from dry areas, and up to three weeks with tropical rainforest species. Remove them from the chamber as

soon as breeding has occurred. Breeding typically occurs in the evening, during or after the artificial rain. Be careful not to overdo the use of rain chambers; tree frogs often become stressed after excessive exposure and succumb to disease. Carefully monitor your frogs, noting their color and skin condition when they are in the rain chamber. If they look off color or ill, immediately return them to normal conditions, particularly if they show no signs of breeding behavior.

Rearing Tadpoles

Tadpoles are very sensitive to water conditions and changes in water conditions. During the first few days after hatching, keep them in the rain chamber tank. They can be transferred to rearing tanks at a later time.

Always use dechlorinated or dechloraminated water when rearing tadpoles. Allow the water to age for at least twenty-four hours before use, so that dissolved gases may escape. With certain species, introducing warm water from the tap into a tank of tadpoles can result in gas-bubble disease. (If the dissolved gases in a liquid are at higher temperature and higher concentration than that of the tadpole's body, they can penetrate its skin and accumulate, forming a subcutaneous gas bubble that usually proves fatal.) Tadpoles that float or cannot swim toward the bottom of their enclosures are usually the victims of gas-bubble disease.

To collect the red-eyed tree frog tadpoles as they drop, place a shallow water container below the egg mass.

Tree frog tadpoles require large tanks with aged high-quality water in order to survive. Keep the pH of the water slightly alkaline, normally ranging between 7.2 and 7.4 for most species. Only a few species can tolerate acidic water. If you have greenhouse facilities, use children's wading pools, readily available in department stores, or plastic watering troughs, such as those produced by Rubbermaid, for tadpole rearing or conditioning water. The authors add carbon-filtered water, water hyacinth, and water lettuce to these troughs. The plants maintain high water quality while the tadpoles are growing, and later provide climbing areas for emerging froglets. Whenever you change tadpole water, attempt to match the temperature of the existing water and to maintain a purity and pH similar to that of the original water. Spread your tadpoles into several tanks and keep them at moderate densities (five per gallon) to increase your chances of success.

Indoors, the best filtering systems are air pump driven biological foam filters. Their design allow keepers to easily clean filters, at the same time preventing the risk of tadpoles being sucked into a motor-driven filter. If packed with enough floss that tadpoles cannot become trapped, box filters are also a safe option. Undergravel filters also work, but they may become overloaded with biological waste.

Aquatic plants, if provided with enough light, are also beneficial, and certain leafy species are sometimes eaten by the tadpoles. Heat the tadpole rearing tanks with submersible heaters and, if you keep your tadpoles indoors, light them with overhead, fluorescent full-spectrum lighting for twelve to fourteen hours per day.

Feeding Tadpoles

Most tree frog tadpoles will feed on commercial fish diets. As a rule, basic fish flakes, such as Tetramin and flakes containing spirulina, are good food sources for tree frog tadpoles. Sera Micron, a powdered algae-containing diet, is a worthwhile dietary supplement, particularly for small tadpoles. Use a varied diet whenever possible, and do not overfeed your tadpoles. Overfeeding may foul the water and, therefore, threaten their lives. Usually, a light feeding two or three times daily will result in rapid growth. Monitor water conditions and change water as needed.

Water Tests

Aspiring frog breeders often complain that their tadpoles suddenly started dying in mass. The usual reason for this phenomenon is that, as tadpoles grow larger and eat more, more wastes are produced even though conditions look the same. Sudden, large-scale tadpole deaths are usually the result of changes in water quality, often a build up of nitrates and ammonia. Besides regular 10 percent partial water changes (once or twice a week in most cases), test the water on a regular basis for ammonia and pH. If using the pool rearing method (adding water simply when needed), you also should test the water for hardness.

Metamorphosing Froglets

Tadpole growth begins with an increase in overall size; next their hind limbs emerge, followed by their forelimbs; finally, the head and mouth change into a froglet mouth. During this process the tadpoles reabsorb their tail. Once the tadpoles become froglets, they will exhaust themselves and drown if they do not have access to climbing areas. At that time, it is critical to provide climbing areas that offer easy access from the water to surface plants. Plants that grow well in water, such as arrowhead plants, pothos, and Chinese evergreen, work in indoor setups, but you also can use partially submerged rocks, freshwater driftwood, or acrylic or glass ramps attached with silicone to the bottom of the enclosure. Just make sure that you provide a climbing area that allows froglets to leave the water.

Handling

Tree frogs are meant to be observed, not handled. Frogs do not like to be petted by dry, rough human hands, and experts do not recommend frequent handling. If you need to touch your frogs for any reason, wash and wet your hands with clean water. Some of the calmer tree frogs may climb and rest on your hand, but most species will not remain in place for any length of time and will eventually jump off. The exception to this rule is White's tree frogs, particularly adult specimens, which tend to be placid and will remain on a hand for long periods without any intentions of jumping. Because of its placid temperament and its hardy constitution, many experts consider White's tree frog to be the best pet tree frog.

Do not allow children to handle frogs without parental supervision. Not only will the frogs escape from young hands, but there are also hygiene issues associated with frog handling. Make sure that any children who come into contact with your frogs do not to put their fingers in their mouths or rub their eyes during or after handling. In addition, have them wash their hands immediately after handling any frog, preferably with a bactericidal soap.

CHAPTER 6
WHITE'S TREE FROGS

Herpetoculturists often call amphibians and reptiles by their scientific names to avoid any confusion about the species in question. The scientific name of White's tree frogs is *Litoria caerulea*, and they are members of the Pelodryadinaea subfamily of the large family of tree frogs called Hylidae. The species name *caerulea* means "blue," a name that is presumably attributed to the color of preserved specimens, but most wild White's tree frogs are actually green. Occasionally, captive-bred White's tree frogs metamorphose with a bluish skin that becomes more blue as they mature. Captive-raised specimens maintained under low lighting also tend to lose the typical green coloration and become blue-green to blue.

The common name, "White's tree frogs," refers to the naturalist who first described the species. In the pet trade, White's tree frogs are sold under a variety of names, usually

A greenhouse-raised White's tree frog. When raised indoors without exposure to natural light, these frogs often become bluish or brownish blue.

White's tree frogs, dumpy tree frogs, or Australian or Indonesian dumpy tree frogs (this name is dependant on their origin).

Distribution

White's tree frogs are found in northern and eastern Australia, islands in the Torres Straits, New Guinea, and New Zealand (where they are an introduced species).

Size

Large female White's tree frogs can reach a snout-to-vent length of 4 inches; males are usually smaller.

Longevity

The oldest specimen on record was twenty-one years old and still living at the time its age was reported. With a reasonable amount of care, captive-bred and -raised animals can live ten years or more.

Sexing

It can be difficult to determine the sex of White's tree frogs, particularly when dealing with younger animals. The most reliable method is to observe your frogs until the males begin calling (which they do by the age of one year), then isolate the males. If you do not have the facilities to isolate the frogs, you can sex individual frogs by examining their feet. To do this, place your index and middle finger across the frog's back and your thumb along its belly and chest area. Once it is firmly in hand, check the inside of its thumbs. Males in varying degrees of breeding condition have small brown "nuptial pads" on the inside of their feet. If the frog is not in breeding condition, its nuptial pads will be so faint that they will be almost impossible to distinguish.

There are a few other methods you can use to determine the sex of your specimens. With mature males, slightly pressing your the thumb against its chest area will sometimes elicit a call or partial call. (Remember, this means applying only gentle pressure.) Another less reliable option is to examine the skin of the throat just before the "fold" line

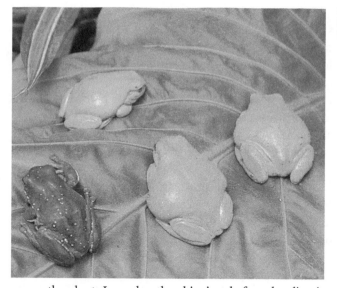

across the chest. In males, the skin just before that line is often looser and slightly more gray than in females. Ultimately, calling and sexual behavior are the best indicators of your frogs' sex.

Varieties of White's Tree Frogs

Herpetologists usually do not recognize varieties or forms of White's tree frogs based on characteristics that are selectively bred or associated with frogs from different areas.

Only two major distinctions are made by herpetoculturists, depending on the tree frog's area of origin: the original Australian White's tree frog, and the more recently imported Indonesian White's tree frog. Most commercial breeders have tried to keep these varieties isolated.

Australian White's tree frogs are characterized primarily by their bright green, blue-green, or turquoise-blue coloration. As a rule, the thick glandular supratympanic (ridge that runs over the ear) ridge in this variety is slight to moderate. Breeders of Australian specimens have recently attempted to produce highly white-spotted strains, a blue strain, and a pseudo-*splendida* strain, which combines large yellow-white spots on the back with the toad-like glands characteristic of *L. splendida*.

39

Indonesian White's tree frogs are often a dull green. The supratympanic ridge varies from slight to extreme, in which case fatty development can nearly cover their eyes. These frogs can vary in size from small to quite large. Females commonly develop greater glandular supratympanic ridges than males. Little selective breeding has been done with Indonesian White's tree frogs, but the large gene pool available should offer future opportunities for the development of interesting new strains.

Housing and Maintenance

House White's tree frogs in tall, all-glass vivaria with screen tops. Juveniles can be housed in vivaria as small as a standard 5- or 10-gallon aquarium but will require a larger enclosure within a year. The minimum enclosure size for adult White's tree frogs is a standard 20-gallon, tall vivarium, but experts recommend at least a standard 29-gallon tank. Standard 10-gallon vivaria are not tall enough for adequate display of adults and seriously limit their natural level of activity. On the other hand, certain custom 18-gallon tall vivaria are ideal for small numbers of this species. If you plan to display a large number of frogs, or desire a more aesthetically pleasing tank, use a larger and taller vivarium.

If you use a large vivarium (40 gallons or more) to house a group of White's tree frogs, you can create a water area by attaching a pre-cut piece of glass to the bottom and sides of the enclosure with silicone adhesive. Proper water maintenance of this area requires regular cleaning and siphoning. In a very large vivarium (60 gallons or more), you can use a water pump to create a miniature waterfall. The water pump also allows you to run the water through a filtering medium (which can be as simple as filter pads or aquarium filter floss) to facilitate cleaning and siphoning.

Ground Media

From a purely practical point of view, newspaper, plain newsprint, or brown paper are all acceptable substrates for White's tree frogs. Experts recommend this medium for dealers and stores that house large numbers of frogs. Such media are inexpensive and allow for regular and easy replacement, thus reducing possible outbreaks of disease as a result of bacterial growth or toxins.

For display purposes, you have two better choices. One, recommended only for use in larger vivaria (29 gallons or more), consists of a 2-inch layer of a peat-based potting soil (one that does not contain perlite or added fertilizers) over a layer of 1 to 1½ inches of pea gravel or coarse aquarium gravel. This mixture allows keepers to create a planted vivarium if they desire.

The other option is to use 1 to 1½ inches of medium-grade orchid bark at the bottom of the vivarium. Decorate these vivaria with selected pieces of wood, rocks, and potted plants concealed by vivarium landscape elements.

Some people also place orchid bark over ground media for decorative purposes and to reduce the surface moisture of the ground medium. Make sure the bark remains dry and that you use fir-based bark, not cedar.

Screen Covers

Your tree frogs' vivarium should have a tightly fitting screen cover, preferably one with a locking mechanism. Do not use a solid glass cover or a cover with only a few ventilation holes; White's tree frogs require good ventilation in order to thrive, and at least 50 percent of the cover should allow for free air flow. A poorly designed cover can lead to escape and the eventual discovery of a dust-covered, dried out, frog-shaped mummy.

Landscaping the Vivarium

In large vivaria with potting soil as a primary ground medium, you can use a number of elements to create an attractive vivarium. When placed near the back of the vivarium, slabs of cork bark provide an interesting background as well as vertical shelters and climbing areas for White's tree frogs. Cork bark is sold in pet stores that specialize in reptiles. The best plants to place in front of the cork bark are broad-leafed snakeplants (*Sansevieria* spp.). They are often available in the houseplant sections of supermarkets, and they are almost always available from nurseries specializing in houseplants. The most readily available types are the variegated *S. trifasciata* and *S. "Moonshine,"* a very attractive, pale green, broad-leafed cultivar. Sansevierias are tough plants, capable of surviving the abuse of active White's tree frogs. They require moderate to strong light and moderate watering, but soggy soil will cause the roots and, eventually, the entire plant to rot, so keep this in mind when you water the ground medium.

In the foreground, add freshwater driftwood or small, curled pieces of cork bark as climbing areas for the frogs. Place only one or two pieces diagonally inside the vivarium; these frogs need room to move, so creating any kind of tangle is undesirable.

White's tree frogs do everything with vigor, including moving about the vivarium. This makes selecting foreground plants for their vivaria a difficult task. They will usually end up crushing any thin-leafed or soft-stemmed species you introduce. In very large vivaria, the cut-leaf philodendron (*Monstera deliciosa*) usually manages to survive because its thick stems withstand any permanent damage and its broad leaves will either support a White's tree frog or cause it to fall. In smaller vivaria, resign yourself to a tank without foreground plants, except a few low plants or ground covers. Good choices for this purpose are the bird's nest Sansevieria (*S.t. "Hahnii"*) and some of the spineless bromeliads.

When you use orchid bark as a ground medium, you can use all of the forementioned plants, but you should add them in plastic pots, partially buried in the ground medium, and concealed and held in place by landscape structures.

Water

White's tree frogs need clean, available water at all times. Thus, you should introduce water in a large porcelain bowl or a glass dish, or, if you have a built-in water area, in the water section of your vivarium. Keep the water depth no higher than the height of your White's tree frogs (legs folded) when at rest. For juveniles, place a small rock in the

A naturalistic vivarium suitable for tree frogs.

water bowl to allow the frogs to climb in and out easily. Many juvenile White's tree frogs drown in water bowls or dishes with excessively deep water or steep sides, so take every precaution to prevent this.

In some areas of the United States, keepers have had difficulty keeping White's tree frogs alive, even though they are fairly easy to maintain. Check the quality of the water you put in the tank. For juveniles, it is a good idea to dechlorinate the water by using the standard dechlorinators sold in the fish trade. If you have any doubts about the quality of your tap water, use bottled drinking water—definitely not distilled water. White's tree frogs do best in water that is slightly alkaline and moderately hard.

Temperature

White's tree frogs require temperatures between 76–85 °F. At night, they safely tolerate temperature drops to 65 °F. You can use several methods to heat a White's tree frog vivarium. During the day, you can place low-wattage incandescent bulbs over select basking areas—usually part of a branch or slab of bark—so that the highest temperature of the area nearest to the light is 85 °F.

Other methods preferred by herpetoculturists consist of using heat cables on a rheostat, heat strips, or heating pads beneath the vivarium. Some use submersible heaters in a water area or in jars. "Hot rocks" are not suitable for White's tree frogs because their surface temperature is too high. At night, if you have no other heat source available, use a low-wattage red incandescent bulb to heat the tank.

Whatever heating system you use, carefully calibrate the temperature so that it is within the proper range. Make sure to read the instructions before using any heating system in order to prevent electrocution or fires.

Other Lighting

To maintain plants and light your frogs' vivarium, experts recommend full-spectrum fluorescent bulbs, such as the VitaLite. Full-spectrum bulbs allow your plants to flourish and bring out the natural colors of animals and in plants. In a smaller vivarium, experts recommend at least one fluorescent bulb running its length; for larger ones, use two or more. Without proper lighting, plants will etiolate (grow pale and thin) and eventually be crushed by your frogs.

If you cannot afford fluorescent lighting, don't worry; White's can be maintained in a plantless vivarium, receiving only bright indirect light from a window. Just make sure that you do not place your vivarium in direct sunlight, which can result in cooked tree frogs during a bright summer day.

Maintaining the Vivarium

As you will soon discover, any frog with the spunk and energy of a White's tree frog can make a mess of a vivarium in no time. White's tree frogs eat large amounts of food and consequently defecate copiously, usually, but not always, in the water area, which therefore needs regular cleaning and replacement. White's also may defecate on various select areas in the vivarium, such as plants and wood. In a large vivarium, daily misting in the early evening can help keep most of these areas clean.

White's tree frogs also tend to smear varying amounts of their skin mucus on the sides of the glass, and regular misting can also help keep the glass free of buildup. Despite regular mistings, every couple of weeks it is necessary to spray the sides of the vivarium with water and use a plastic scrub pad or single-edged razor to rub off the thin coat of mucus. Finish up the cleaning with a moist paper towel to restore the viewing clarity of the glass.

Feeding White's Tree Frogs

White's tree frogs require a proper feeding regimen and correct vitamin and mineral supplementation to survive. As juveniles, White's tree frogs need high levels of calcium to meet the demands of their rapidly growing skeletal system. With insufficient calcium, froglets die or, when treated too late, develop into adults with varying degrees of skeletal deformities.

Feeding juveniles (½ to 1½ inches): Offer two- to three-week-old crickets (they should be no longer than the length of a froglet's head) once a day by placing them near your froglets. Twice a week, coat the crickets with a reptile multivitamin supplement and calcium carbonate (one part supplement to every three parts calcium).

It is important that you feed your froglets in the proper manner. If they do not consume the crickets soon after they are introduced, most of the supplements on the crickets will fall off and you may end up with calcium deficient frogs. It is better to feed White's tree frogs at night, when they are more likely to be active, than during the daytime, when they are usually asleep in their shelters.

Feeding sub-adults and adults (1½ to 3 inches): Every two to three days, feed three- to four-week-old crickets to your older frogs. Coat the crickets with a supplement/calcium mix (as previously mentioned) once a week. If your frogs will eat one- or two-day-old "pink" mice, offer one every two to four weeks. If you think your frog may not be getting enough calcium from the crickets, dip the rump of the feeder mouse in calcium.

Feeding adults: Two to three times per week, feed adult frogs large crickets; occasionally, you can feed them an early-stage "fuzzy" mouse. To prevent problems associated with excessive calcium intake, supplement crickets and other insects only one time each week. If you want your frogs to live a long time, monitor their diets and do not allow them to become obese. Fat White's tree frogs may look cute and dumpy, or bizarre because of extensive supratympanic glandular development, but excessive fat reserves make them more prone to disease and often shorten their life spans.

Breeding

If properly maintained, captive-raised Australian White's tree frogs reach sexual maturity in their second year. For breeding purposes, select only healthy adult pairs with good weight. Precondition them for breeding during the cool months (ideally late winter) by placing them in a clean, partially covered, sterile vivarium in a cool area of your facility, and exposing them to temperatures of 65 °F for as many as sixteen hours per day. Keep the vivarium in the dark and provide vertical shelters. Do not offer any food during this time.

Cool your tree frogs with this method for six weeks before attempting to breed them. Following the cooling period, maintain them under optimal conditions with adequate heat, and feed them regularly for two to four weeks.

The next step is to induce breeding. Place your tree frogs in a large aquarium or another large enclosure with 3 to 4 inches of aged, high-quality water, and add water plants, such as Anachris and water hyacinth, and floating foam platforms. Using a water pump, construct a rain chamber by running water through a large plastic container with multiple holes drilled in it, or through drilled PVC pipe with a capped end (see "Building a Rain

Chamber" in Captive Breeding). Make sure that a screen covers the top of the vivarium to prevent escape. Introduce the frogs and set the rain chamber on a timer so that it rains from 6 to 10 PM. Breeding usually occurs after two to five days of this schedule, during the dry phase of the rain chamber. Females typically lay several thousand eggs. After breeding occurs, remove the adult frogs, turn off the rain chamber, and add an air-stone (connected to an air pump) in the water (air-stones are available in any pet store that has aquarium equipment). At a temperature of 80–85° F, frogs begin hatching in twenty-eight to thirty-six hours. After hatching, tadpoles become inactive and rest on the bottom of the tank; within twenty-four to thirty-six hours, this changes and they start clinging to the sides of the vivarium and plants.

Rearing tadpoles requires several hundred gallons of aged, high-quality water (dechlorinated, dechloramined, and allowed to sit long enough for most water-dissolved gasses to dissipate) maintained at a temperature of 80–85 °F. Make sure the tanks receive natural sunlight (if in a greenhouse or in a warm area) or light from full-spectrum fluorescent lights, and that you keep live plants in the vivarium water. Breeders often have the most success when they raise White's tree frogs in large pools with live plants and natural light, not under sterile laboratory conditions.

On the fourth day after hatching, begin feeding the tadpoles a high-quality tropical fish flake food twice per day. During the rearing stage, keep the water reasonably clean and the tadpoles away from crowded conditions (a maximum of 15 tadpoles per gallon of water). You must continue to maintain the quality of the water; as always, make sure that it is dechlorinated, dechloraminated, and aged.

The first metamorphosing frogs emerge during the fourth week, and metamorphosis will extend for several weeks. Provide plants or platforms for the emerging froglets, or they will drown. The biggest challenge of breeding White's tree frogs is providing housing and maintenance for hundreds or thousands of froglets. Under overcrowded conditions, the froglet mortality rate will be very high.

Ideally, you should provide large screen enclosures or screen houses.

After housing considerations, you must figure out how to feed hundreds or thousands of froglets with high food requirements, which can be expensive as well as time consuming. For private breeders who wish simply to raise a small number of White's tree frogs, it is wisest to limit the number of froglets that you accommodate at the tadpole stage. When raising larger numbers of froglets, houseflies are an inexpensive dietary component.

CHAPTER 7

NOTES ON POPULAR SPECIES

White-lipped Tree Frogs (*Litoria infrafrenata*)

Until the recent glut of imported Indonesian white-lipped tree frogs, herpetoculturists used to dream of being able to own this species. Like White's tree frogs, white-lipped tree frogs are large and beautiful, and are best displayed in attractive vivaria. Unlike the more manageable White's tree frog, however, this restless species cannot readily be handled and secretes a sticky whitish mucus when handled excessively. They are also more delicate and less tolerant to cold than White's tree frogs. They are usually sold under the common name white-lipped tree frogs, but some dealers sell them as Indonesian giant green tree frogs.

An Australian white-lipped tree frog.

Size
Large females grow as big as 5 inches; males are smaller.

Distribution
White-lipped tree frogs range throughout Cape York Peninsula and Queensland, Australia; New Guinea; New Ireland, Bismarck Archipelago; and were introduced into Java.

Longevity
The authors have kept white-lipped tree frogs, obtained as adults, for six years, which were still alive at the time they were sold. They can probably survive for at least ten years in captivity.

Sexing
Males are smaller than females, and their throat is darker and has looser skin. Mature males ready to breed have dark nuptial pads on the inside of their thumbs.

Variation
White-lipped tree frogs are available in a number of varieties. Large Australia specimens, which have a finely textured, bright green skin, and orange immediately behind their arms, are the most attractive. The white-lipped tree frogs currently being imported from Indonesia can vary a great deal. The most attractive specimens have bright green coloration and broad, pearl-white margins along their hindlegs, while the least attractive are a dull, dark green. In captivity, many white-lipped tree frogs become faded green or blue-green, and some of the Indonesian frogs become a dirty green. The cause of this color loss may be the quality of lighting (those raised in greenhouses are often brighter, as are similarly kept White's tree frogs) or a dietary deficiency.

Care and Maintenance
Maintain white-lipped tree frogs in a manner similar to that given for White's tree frogs, but keep the temperature above

the lower ranges. They also require higher relative humidity, which you can provide by covering up to half of the vivarium enclosure and giving them a light misting each evening.

Breeding
Use conditions similar to those listed for White's tree frogs, but make sure that nighttime temperatures only drop to 70–74 °F. Froglets of this species are generally more delicate and more difficult to raise than White's tree frogs. Calcium deficiency and varying degrees of skeletal deformity are common among captive-raised white-lipped tree frogs because of inadequate feeding procedures.

Cuban Tree Frog (*Osteopilus septentrionalis*)
Though the Cuban tree frog is an introduced species (not native to this country), it is now well established in southern Florida, and is the largest tree frog found in the United States.

Size
Males grow 1½ to 3½ inches long and females grow up to 5 inches; larger specimens, though very rare, do exist.

Distribution
Cuban tree frogs are found in southern Florida, Cuba, the

Though not a native species, the Cuban tree frog is the largest tree frog now found in the United States.

Isle of Pines, the Bahamas, and the Cayman Islands. They are also introduced species in Puerto Rico and St. Croix.

Sexing
Males are smaller, with a darker throat and nuptial pads (thicker pads found on a frog's thumbs during breeding season) in breeding.

Care and Maintenance
As long as Cuban tree frogs are kept in warm temperatures (at temperatures in the upper 70s °F to low 80s °F in the day, and in the 70s °F at night), they are relatively easy to keep. They can be maintained like White's tree frogs and will consume larger prey, such as baby mice, when mature.

Breeding
Cuban tree frogs are easy to breed after a slight winter cooling and are very prolific breeders; their egg masses consist of up to 2,000 eggs. Tadpoles hatch in twenty-four to forty-eight hours and can be fed on tropical fish flakes, such as Tetramin staple diet. They typically metamorphose in six to eight weeks and reach sexual maturity by one year. Currently, there are few reasons to captive breed this common and inexpensive frog.

Note
Do not keep this frog with smaller animals—it will make a meal of them. Do not rub your eyes during or after handling Cuban tree frogs; their skin secretions are quite noxious.

Green Tree Frog (*H. cinerea*)
The green tree frog is an attractive, readily available, and easy-to-keep U.S. species.

Size
Specimens grow 1¼ to 2¼ inches.

Distribution
This wide-ranging species is found from Delaware south

along the coastal plain into Florida and west to Texas, north through central Arkansas and western Tennessee to Illinois.

Sexing
Mature males have a darker, dirty-yellow throat.

Variation
Some individuals have a fair amount of golden yellow spotting, while others have wide, silvery-white side stripes that are also very appealing. Both of these unusual variations may be more widespread among certain populations. Selective breeding for yellow spotting and wide stripes could result in some spectacular animals in the future. Recently, collectors found an axanthic specimen that is an intense light blue. It was purchased by Robert Mailloux and has been successfully bred to normal animals. A new generation is in the works and, depending on the genetics of this trait, sky-blue colored green tree frogs may one day be available.

Care and Maintenance
Use the care conditions recommended for White's tree frogs, but make sure to use a naturalistic vivarium. Established

specimens lie on plants and make nice vivarium displays. Males can be noisy, and tend to call whenever a low-pressure system moves in.

Breeding
If cooled in the winter, this species is not difficult to breed. You can keep at least two males and an equal number of females together. Higher temperatures, drops in barometric pressure, and exposure to a rain chamber will condition these frogs for breeding. Each clutch contains about 700 eggs, and females may lay more than one clutch per season. The tadpole stage lasts approximately thirty-five days. Feed a standard fish flake diet to tadpoles and week-old crickets to the tiny froglets. Under optimal conditions, tadpoles reach sexual maturity in less than a year.

Note
In certain areas in the wild, this species hybridizes with the barking tree frog.

Barking Tree Frog (*H. gratiosa*)
The barking tree frog is one of the prettiest and most desirable U.S. species. Its large, squat body, and attractive colors and patterns make it one of the country's most fascinating frogs.

Size
These frogs grow from 2 to 2¼ inches long.

Distribution

Barking tree frogs range from North Carolina to southern Florida and eastern Louisiana. There are also colonies in Delaware, Maryland, Kentucky, Tennessee, and Virginia.

Longevity

If properly maintained, barking tree frogs can live seven years or more.

Sexing

Males have a loose greenish-yellow throat. The majority of animals sold in pet stores are collected during breeding and are males.

Care and Maintenance

Use the same general care conditions listed for White's tree frog. Under optimal conditions—moderate warmth and moderate relative humidity—this species will rest on leaves, sides of the enclosures, and other surfaces. Under less than optimal conditions (too dry, too cool, or too warm), this species will burrow under landscape structures or just beneath the surface of the substrate. In spite of what several other authors have written, the barking tree frog is not always an easy species to keep on a long-

term basis. Collected animals stored in crowded conditions prior to distribution may become infested by parasites, and matching natural climatic cycles and environmental conditions may be necessary for their long-term survival in captivity.

Breeding

This species should be bred commercially. It ranks among the best tree frogs, and it has many of the physical characteristics that make frogs appealing: dumpy appearance, attractive coloration, and good display potential (when they are not hiding). Unfortunately, captive breeding programs for this frog are scarce. But, following a period of cooling, the barking tree frog should breed if it is exposed to rain and decreased barometric pressure.

Gray Tree Frogs (*H. chrysoscelis* and *H. versicolor*)

Gray tree frogs are commonly available in the spring, when they are collected during breeding aggregations. These two species, which are similar in appearance but can be distinguished by their calls (*H. chrysoscelis* make a fast trill, *H. versicolor* call in a slow trill), have an appealing cryptic beauty; they are marbled in gray or with shades of green or a pale, almost white coloration. Their color changes depending on a number of factors, including temperature and exposure to light, but they typically have bright orange and black colors on their thighs. The two species also differ genetically; *H. chrysoscelis* is diploid, whereas *H. versicolor* is tetraploid (twice the number of chromosome pairs).

Size
These frogs grow from 1¼ to 2⅜ inches.

Longevity
Specimens can live seven years or more.

Sexing
Males have a darker yellowish throat.

Care and Maintenance
Keep these pretty display animals under the same conditions listed for White's tree frog, using a naturalistic vivarium. Gray tree frogs fare best when exposed to cooler winter temperatures in the 50s °F and 60s °F (they will tolerate even lower temperatures), at least at night, for one to two months.

Breeding
If they were to become less common, gray tree frogs would be worth breeding. Within their normal distribution range, greenhouse environments with pools set up would work well for large scale breeding.

Note
Gray tree froglets often flutter the middle digits of their hind legs when feeding.

Golden Foam Nest Frogs (*Polypedates leucomystax*)
Golden foam nest frogs used to be imported regularly from Southeast Asia. If healthy when first obtained, they are hardy, long-lived, and easy to breed. Large females can have an attractive golden color.

Size
Males grow up to 2¾ inches; large females can be as large as four inches long.

Distribution
Golden foam nest frogs are native to Southeast Asia.

Longevity
Specimens can live for six years or more.

Sexing
Females are often larger than males.

Care and Maintenance
Use most of the guidelines listed for White's tree frog, but keep in mind that this species is not tolerant of low temperatures or low relative humidity. They are best kept in naturalistic tropical-forest vivaria with daytime temperatures in the upper 70s °F to low 80s °F. Keep the temperature above the low 70s °F. Once established, these frogs make good display animals.

Breeding
Under the dry/wet-cycle (alternating simulated dry and rainy seasons) method, this species breeds readily in

A gliding tree frog.

captivity. The female creates foam nests and lays about 175 eggs, which hatch in three to four days, and may lay several clutches each year. Place a container of water below the eggs so that the tadpoles will fall into the water when they hatch. Raise the tadpoles on tropical fish flake food. They will metamorphose between one and three months, and you can use standard tadpole-rearing methods to rear the froglets.

Gliding Tree Frogs (*Rhacophorus nigropalmatus* and *R. rheinwardtii*)

The brightly colored webbing and sides of these large Asian tree frogs mark them as one of the most beautiful species available. Unfortunately, imported specimens are usually thin, weak, and highly parasitized, and many have varying numbers of dorsal sores.

Size
Specimens grow up to 3½ inches long.

Care and Maintenance
Captive collections of these frogs often have a high mortality rate, though, by adhering to the procedures listed in this book, you should have some success raising them in captivity. Flagyl and Baytril treatment, combined with hand feeding, can work miracles on unhealthy animals. Once established, keep these species under the conditions listed for red-eyed tree frogs. Experts recommend larger plants, such as Chinese evergreens, as perching and possible breeding areas.

Breeding

Although they are not bred in captivity (to our knowledge), keepers should make every effort to establish captive populations of these beautiful tree frogs. Breeding information is not yet available, but gliding tree frogs probably require breeding conditions similar to those listed for red-eyed tree frogs or foam nest frogs.

Australian Red-Eyed Tree Frog (*Litoria chloris*)

Large dealers offered froglets captive-bred by European herpetoculturists about fifteen years ago, but there are reports of animals being offered in the early 1980s. Since then, captive-bred froglets of this species have been intermittently available. The authors have bred this species on a number of occasions, and they are becoming more available to pet keepers. (At least 1,000 froglets now are offered through the pet trade every year.) Although not as attractive as Central American red-eyed tree frogs, these frogs have bright yellow-orange hands and feet, and their eyes have orange- or red-edged irises. It is probable that some Australian populations have more intense red coloration in their irises than others.

Size

Specimens grow up to 2½ inches long.

Distribution

These tree frogs are native to Australia.

Sexing

Males have a yellowish throat and are slightly smaller than females.

Care and Maintenance

These tree frogs can be maintained and bred under conditions similar to those listed for White's tree frogs, but they are generally less tolerant of low relative humidity and temperature extremes than White's tree frogs.

Breeding

Keep this species slightly cooler and drier for eight weeks, then introduce them into a rain chamber; they will breed readily. Some keepers have obtained as many as five clutches in an extended breeding season by placing pairs in a rain chamber every four weeks. Females lay approximately 500 eggs per clutch. They should be well fed and kept relatively dry between clutches. The tadpoles hatch in two days and are easily raised on Tetramim Staple tropical fish flakes. Froglets emerge after four weeks and, under optimal rearing conditions, become sexually mature by nine months.

CHAPTER 8

RED-EYED TREE FROGS

By Drew W. Ready

The rain forests of Central America are home to some of the most interesting and beautiful plants and animals on earth. Amazingly, one of the most magnificent creatures living among the orchids, bromeliads, broad-leafed plants, and tangles of tropical vines is also one of the smallest, an amphibian known as the red-eyed tree frog (*A. callidryas*).

Originally described as *Agalychnis callidryas* by Cope in 1862, its scientific name clearly matches its extraordinary nature. *Callidryas*, its species name, is a derivative of the Greek words *kallos*, meaning "beautiful," and *dryas*, meaning "tree nymph," thereby christening it the beautiful tree nymph of the rain forest.

A newly metamor-phosed Australian red-eye tree frog resting in foliage.

Few dealers imported red-eyed tree frogs before the mid to late 1980s, when U.S. importers began receiving regular shipments of reptiles and amphibians from Honduras. The shipments came in by the hundreds, carrying hundreds of other species, including forest chameleons, cone headed lizards, emerald swifts, masked tree frogs, turnip tail geckos, and palm salamanders, many of which became available to the general public through the pet trade.

Finally, in the late 1980s, all Honduran reptile shipments ceased, and within two years, very few red-eyed tree frogs remained in captivity. Two primary reasons precipitated this: a lack of detailed, high-quality husbandry information; and neglect. By 1990, of the thousands of frogs imported from Honduras, less than a hundred remained in U.S. collections.

Fortunately for frog enthusiasts, red-eyed tree frogs are occasionally shipped to the United States from several regions in Central America, and better yet, they are being bred in captivity in unprecedented numbers.

Taxonomy

The red-eyed tree frog is a member of the family Hylidae, of the order Anura, within the class Amphibia. The family Hylidae, which contains all true tree frogs, is made up of many subfamilies. Red-eyed tree frogs are classified in the subfamily Phyllomedusinae, in which there are six genera and forty-two recognized species. Red-eyed tree frog share their genus, *Agalychnis*, with seven other species.

Agalychnis callidryas' dark blue or brown flanks with vertical white to yellow bars distinguish it from all other species of its genus. As of now, *A. callidryas* is the only species of this genus that is regularly imported for the pet trade in the United States.

Description

Males reach a maximum snout-to-vent length of 2.2 inches, and females, which are larger, can reach a length of more than 2.5 inches. Their color and size vary, depending on geographic location. Red-eyes from the northernmost part of their range (Southern Mexico and Guatemala) are the smallest and usually display light blue flanks; those from more southern parts (Nicaragua and Costa Rica) tend to be larger in size and display dark blue flanks. The red-eyed tree frog's dorsum (back) is green, but the shade varies based on the geographic location of the specimen. Some red-eyed tree frogs have small white spots on their dorsal surface. Their venters (bellies) are creamy white, and their feet are shades of yellow to orange. The vertical pupil is uncommon in the eyes of hylids, but all members of the Phyllomedusine subfamily exhibit the same characteristic. Researchers theorize that the brilliant coloration, or flash markings, of this species exist to startle and ward off predators.

Distribution

The red-eyed tree frog is found from southern Mexico south to eastern Panama. It dwells in tropical lowland rain forest, although it has also been found on the upward slopes of tropical mountain regions. Because of the massive destruction of Central American rain forest habitat and the recent decline of many amphibian populations, it is not known whether or not these frogs still exist in areas defined by previous type localities.

Behavioral Characteristics

Red-eyed tree frogs are primarily arboreal and nocturnal, sleeping in the forest canopy during the day, and displaying their colors and hunting for food at night. They are considered to be exclusively insectivorous, taking advantage of the huge abundance of insects in the forest canopy. As the light of morning approaches, the frogs search out a resting spot— a palm frond, a Philodendron leaf, or a bromeliad—to call home for the day. Once they have found a suitable site, they bring in their arms and legs tight to their bodies, close their eyes, and do their best to blend in with the foliage.

Breeding occurs at the onset of the rainy season. As depressions in the ground fill up with rain water and form small pools, red-eyed tree frogs descend from the canopy to find a mate. From branches and vines above these tempo-

rary ponds, males emit a series of calls in anticipation of attracting responsive females. Once a female approaches a male, or a male finds a female, he climbs on her back and proceeds to clasp her. If the female is receptive, she searches for a suitable site (or sites) in which to deposit her eggs. Usually, the female selects a large leaf a few feet above the water, but clutches of eggs have also been found on vines, branches, and tree trunks above or near water.

The female releases the eggs in a gelatinous mass, and they are fertilized by the male clinging to her back. On average, clutches contain about fifty eggs, although experts have witnessed clutches of fourteen to one-hundred and eight eggs. The developing tadpoles wriggle about, rupture the enveloping membrane, and fall into the water within six to ten days. The tadpoles forage for food in the pool and complete metamorphosis in forty to eighty days. The emerging froglets are usually brownish in color and lack the characteristic red pigment in their eyes. The striking colors become apparent as the tree frog develops.

Selecting Healthy Tree Frogs

When you first see a red-eyed tree frog, you may find it very difficult to resist the impulse to purchase the animal without taking the steps necessary to make sure that the frog is in good health and has not succumbed to the stresses of captivity. Unless you acquire the appropriate equipment and know-how, your frog will not survive long.

By the time most wild-caught amphibians reach a dealer, they have traveled through many hands, leaving the animals stressed and malnourished. Select frogs that have no visible discoloration and have a healthy body weight; bone outlines should not be visible. Because they are typically shipped in small containers, many frogs arrive with snout damage. Avoid any frogs with raw, badly damaged snouts (and possibly suggest that they be treated immediately by the dealer).

Examine the entire animal, looking for any signs of infection. Sick animals appear thin and are often awake during daylight hours. It is best to purchase captive-bred amphibians whenever possible. They lack the parasites found in wild-caught animals, and there is no need to acclimate them to captivity. Captive-bred stock are now more prevalent in pet stores than they ever have been.

Sexing

When selecting specimens from a large group, sexing the red-eyed tree frog is a fairly easy task. Among adults, males are much smaller than females. With juveniles and froglets, your chances seem to depend on the luck of the draw, although some females can be determined by their more truncated snouts.

Housing

It is extremely important to properly acclimatize your frogs to captivity. Animals taken from the wild do not acclimate well to small enclosures. Use a tall, 30-gallon terrarium to create a vivarium that provides a small group of red-eyed tree frogs with the space they need. Custom-built vivaria for arboreal frogs are even better. Your vivarium should have a half-glass and half-screen top to assure adequate ventilation and proper humidity. Never house red-eyed tree frogs in anything smaller than a tall 20-gallon terrarium. Other authors have suggested smaller setups, but tree frogs need space, especially vertical space, and animals housed in smaller vivaria may eventually succumb to the stresses of confinement.

Temperature

The optimum temperature for red-eyed tree frogs ranges between 60–85 °F. Constant exposure to the extremes of this range may cause health problems.

There are two common ways to keep the enclosure within the required temperature range. The first is to keep the room in which the animals are housed within an ambient temperature range, thereby assuring that the vivarium remains at the desired temperatures. Because some rooms experience temperature fluctuations or become too cool or too hot, directly heating and cooling the setup is a better method.

When attempting the second heating method, under-the-tank heat elements work very well. If this is not convenient for you, or if the heaters do not supply enough heat, place low-wattage incandescent light bulbs outside the enclosure to increase the temperature. Low-wattage ceramic heat elements that can be screwed into normal incandescent fixtures also provide a good source of heat. Keep the heat source several inches from the top of the vivarium.

Keeping a room adequately cool in the summer months also poses problems for some tree frog enthusiasts. Do not allow vivaria to get direct sunlight in the warmer months. Keeping the shades (blinds, shutters, or draperies) closed and the windows open in the frogs' room will greatly reduce the ambient temperature. If vivarium temperatures rise above 90 °F, turn off the lights (even fluorescent lighting can raise the temperature of a vivarium). Turn lights on again after the heat of the day has passed. If necessary, use small utility fans to circulate cooler air into the vivarium, and occasionally mist the enclosure to reduce the temperature.

Humidity

Maintain the vivarium's humidity levels between 30 and 50 percent during the dry cycle (not when inducing breeding). Constant humidity levels higher than 80 percent can cause health problems for your frogs. Once you have provided a proper water section (see below) and half-screen, half-glass top, simply give the vivarium a light misting a couple of times each week to maintain the proper humidity level.

Water

To create a small water area, section off a corner of the vivarium with a small piece of glass attached with aquarium silicone; otherwise keep a water dish accessible at all times. It is essential that the frogs always have access to clean water. At night, red-eyes find their way to the water and sit with their posteriors submerged in order to hydrate themselves. Most tap water is potentially toxic to frogs; therefore, do not use tap water unless it has been filtered extensively.

Dechlorinate and dechloramine any water before putting it in the tank. Use the product Amquel (available in most aquarium stores) to dechlorinate the water, or allow it to sit for at least twenty-four hours. Bottled or filtered water (or a combination of the two) works best. Change the water in red-eyed tree frog vivaria frequently because the frogs naturally defecate and urinate in the water section. Experts recommend against filtration devices because they do not keep the water as clean as regular water changes. Keep in mind that a simple and natural setup is the key to good vivarium design.

Plants for Vivarium Design

As stated earlier, when building an enclosure for your tree frogs, the best design strategy is to create a naturalistic vivarium. Simulating the animals' natural habitat has long been known to ease the stress of captivity and facilitate acclimation. We recommend starting with a 3- to 5-inch substrate of orchid bark. The vivarium is best landscaped with broad-leafed plants of the aroid family, including Philodendron, *Anthurium*, and *Monstera* species. You can find these plants at most good nurseries and can obtain more exotic species through specialty greenhouses and mail-order nurseries that specialize in tropical plants.

Planted terrariums are also an option, but you must make good drainage available. Leave plants in their pots and sink them into the bark substrate to allow for easy maintenance—even with the pots, the vivarium will still resemble a little rain forest. You can also mount slabs of cork bark on the side of the vivarium by attaching a piece of string to the back side of the cork (as you would a framed picture) and then hanging the cork from suction-cup mounts (found at most nurseries and hardware stores) stuck to the glass. This design element is aesthetically pleasing and makes the vivarium resemble a treelike dwelling. The more you understand about the habitat of your frogs, the better you can meet their needs in captivity.

Lighting

It is still not known whether full-spectrum lighting is a necessity for these nocturnal tree frogs. However, vivarium plants must have lighting that replicates natural sunlight. Full-spectrum fluorescent bulbs provide plants with the needed spectrum of light. Because one bulb is seldom sufficient for many plants, two or more fluorescent bulbs are optimal.

Give your red-eyed tree frogs a light cycle of twelve hours on and twelve hours off. You can accomplish this by using appliance timers, which are available at most hardware stores, or doing it manually. Automation allows for a more exact light cycle and saves you the task of turning your lights off and on every day. Use a dark blue or red incandescent light bulb at night to observe these amazing creatures as they move about the enclosure. In the cooler months, use low-wattage (approximately 25 watts) full-spectrum incandescent bulbs to add light and warmth, but be careful to avoid harmful temperatures.

Feeding

Crickets, a staple diet for many captive reptiles and amphibians, make an excellent diet for red-eyed tree frogs. Although crickets as a key source of nutrition are an acceptable choice, you must still vary your tree frogs' diet. For years, I have fed crickets and houseflies to my frogs without problems, but I follow a few additional steps to assure that my frogs receive proper nutrition. As described in an earlier chapter, you must first nutrient-load store-bought crickets. Store them in a 10-gallon aquarium or a similar container. Place egg crates and torn brown bags in the container for crickets to hide in and defecate on. Feed the crickets a variety of foods, especially carrots, kale, oranges, monkey chow, trout chow, chicken mash, and pulverized fish foods (as small percent of the total diet).

When offering your frogs the crickets, dust the insects once a week with high-quality vitamin and calcium supplements, available from most reptile and amphibian dealers. Rather than letting the crickets run free in the vivarium, place them in bowls or similar containers. This method keeps the supplements on the crickets longer, keeps them out of water, and ensures that your frogs do not consume bark, soil, or any other nonfood material when hunting their prey. Most tree frogs have no problem eating from these bowls. Feed your frogs two to three times per week, supplying them with only enough food for a couple of days at each feeding.

Captive Breeding

If you've followed all of the previous husbandry procedures, it likely won't be long before you become interested in breeding your frogs. Most of the time it is best to keep the vivarium environment moderately dry. Lightly mist the enclosure a couple of times each week to assure the ideal humidity. Because you have the ability to manipulate warm-and-cool and wet-and-dry cycles within the vivarium, you can breed red-eyes at various times of the year; however, it is best to avoid any breeding or tadpole-rearing activity during the cold winter months.

The rising temperature and frequent barometric instability of mid to late spring makes it an ideal time to breed this species. Red-eyed tree frogs are more listless and feed less during the cooler winter months. As winter turns to spring and the weather starts to warm up, the frogs become more active and the males may even start calling. Warm temperatures, spring rains, and changes in barometric pressure induce breeding activity, but the frogs will not breed without simulated rain.

Before attempting to breed your frogs, it is important to

make breeding and rearing preparations well in advance. Tall, medium- to large-sized terraria or aquaria are well suited for use as rain chambers. Tall, 30-gallon setups suffice, but experts recommend larger rain chambers, which give the frogs more space.

You can imitate rain in many different ways, but you will get the best results by keeping it simple (see "Rain Chambers" under Captive Breeding). Construct a water section in the rain chamber by separating at least one-third of the setup with a piece of glass siliconed in place. The glass only needs to be 3 or 4 inches high. For more elaborate setups, drill a hole in a piece of glass at the bottom of the water section to allow for drainage and a circulating rain system. Alternatively, you can use a small powerhead-type pump in the water section of the rain chamber. Many pumps can be modified to fit garden misting systems, which create the "rain" that is necessary to induce this species to breed.

Attach an appliance timer to the misting system to create a regular rain schedule. Use gravel or a similar substrate for the land section so that the frogs have a place to rest and escape the rain drenching the setup. Place plants, such as Anthurium, Monstera, Philodendron, and Spathyphylum, which grow well in rain chambers, in the water, but avoid using potted plants because their soil will quickly spoil the water. Position the plant leaves over the water to give searching females an ideal oviposition (egg-laying) site.

Before attempting to breed your frogs, condition them with a high-nutrient feeding to assure your animals are in good health. If the frogs have been kept dry and the winter cold has past, you can easily induce breeding in the spring months. To increase your chances of success, align your breeding attempts with spring storms and decreases and increases in barometric pressure. Setting your chamber to rain from the late afternoon into the late evening (5 to 11 PM) yields the best results.

Amplexus (the frogs' breeding embrace) usually occurs within the first couple of days, but sometimes takes a couple of weeks. Feed the frogs continually, and take care to remove uneaten and dead crickets. Remove all feces as soon as you see any. It is important to check the rain chamber frequently for eggs. Once you find a clutch, place it in a container in which the embryos can develop and the tadpoles can emerge. If clutches are oviposited on leaves, remove the entire leaf and hang it in the container a few inches above the water section. If you find clutches on the glass, remove them and place them on leaves or other suitable sites above the water to incubate like the others.

The optimum temperature for egg incubation is between 74–78 °F. Constant temperatures below 70 °F and in excess of 80 °F may kill the developing embryos. It generally takes from six to nine days for the embryos to develop into tadpoles. When embryonic development is complete, the encapsulated tadpole wriggles its way free, sliding down the leaf into the water. Once the embryos have completely developed into tadpoles, you can assist their emergence with a light misting. After the eggs hatch, remove the tadpoles from their containers and place them in the prepared rearing aquaria.

In order to avoid competition and overcrowding, divide your tadpoles into small groups. Use a series of 10-gallon aquariums containing 3 to 5 inches of water. The rearing containers may either be plumbed together or be kept separated.

Water quality, temperature, and feeding are the three most important factors in raising tadpoles into froglets. Change the water in rearing setups every couple of days to avoid buildup of harmful chemicals, including ammonia and nitrates. If you choose to filter the tank, sponge filters sold at aquarium stores work well. Remember not to use tap water in your rearing aquaria, and remember that you must dechlorinate and dechloramine all tank water.

Keep the rearing tank's water temperature between 74–80 °F. Lower temperatures will cause the tadpoles to develop more slowly, and higher temperatures can be fatal. You can keep the temperature constant with a high-quality aquarium heater with a built-in thermostat.

Feed your tadpoles fish foods, such as Sera Micron and flake foods (which are easily pulverized), two to three times every day. Tadpoles usually complete metamorphosis in thirty to sixty days, although some stragglers may take a little longer.

When their front legs have emerged, your tadpoles will start to climb the side of the glass. At this point, remove the froglets and place them in setups similar to those of the adults, but keep them at slightly more humid levels. Use a simple bare-bottom tank with small potted plants. Frequently mist the enclosure to keep the vulnerable froglets from becoming too dry, but remember that too much humidity leads to bloating (excessive water absorption), which usually results in death. The key to success at this stage is careful observation and proper adjustments when necessary. Keep a small water dish available to the froglets.

As the tadpoles are developing, prepare food for the emerging froglets. You will need large amounts of pin-head to week-old crickets, fruit flies, and other small insects. The froglets will start to feed shortly after the few days it takes them to reabsorb their tails. Give young red-eyed tree frogs vitamin and calcium supplements with their food. Because young frogs grow at different rates and compete for food, house them in small groups according to size.

Froglets grow relative to the volume and frequency of their feedings. As the tree frogs develop, you must change their diet and enclosure to accommodate them. Depending on their rate of growth, young frogs may become sexually mature in as little as one year. Because of the inherent stresses, do not induce breeding until your animals are at least a year-and-a-half old.

CHAPTER 9

DISEASES AND DISORDERS

ealthy frogs can fight off a wide range of potential pathogens. Therefore, in order to minimize the stress on your frogs and to allow their immune system to function properly, you must first provide optimal conditions. To do so, keep your frogs at the relative humidity and temperature range required by their particular species. Make sure the design of their vivarium provides proper substrates, shelters, and plants. It is equally important to select frogs that appear healthy upon purchase. Nonetheless, despite optimal conditions, tree frogs may exhibit symptoms of disease. The common diseases listed below can be readily treated by herpetoculturists or veterinarians.

Obesity

Overfed captive tree frogs can become grossly obese. This is particularly true of White's tree frogs fed too many pink mice or fed too often. As with humans, obese tree frogs have shorter life spans. In White's tree frogs, fatty deposits around the head can become so great that they will cover the eyes and blind the animal. To remedy obesity, gradually cut back on the amount of food you offer your frogs and provide large vivaria that allow the frogs to be active. Plump frogs may look cute but they are not necessarily healthy.

Internal Parasites

Nematodes

If your frogs' feces appear fairly well formed, any weight loss may indicate nematodes. Ideally, you should have a fecal exam performed by a veterinarian, but some keepers have had success by simply treating their frogs with oral doses of fenbendazole (Panacur) at 50 to 75 mg/kg., repeating the treatment in seven days.

Flagellate Protozoans

Runny and/or bloody feces can be caused by flagellate protozoans. Have a fecal exam performed by a veterinarian if possible. Flagellate protozoans can be treated with metronidazole (Flagyl), administered orally and directly in the stomach at a dosage of 50 mg/kg.

Sores and Injuries

Imported tree frogs may have abrasions on their snouts, skin sores, and physical injuries. Herpetologists have had success in treating these problems by injecting enrofloxacin (Baytril) in the ventral area at a dosage of 10 mg/kg, repeated every forty-eight hours for up to two weeks. With imported frogs, experts also recommend administering metronidazole, which is antibiotic to anaerobic bacteria.

Clouded Eyes

Most imported frogs have clouded eyes, a problem often caused by eye trauma, immune-system failure, or absorption of toxins. To treat afflicted frogs, keep them in simple vivaria with paper towel substrate, ventrally injecting enrofloxacin at a dosage of 10 mg/kg every forty-eight hours for up to two weeks.

A poor diet, dirty tank water, or high ammonia and urate levels in the water can also cause clouded eyes. Make sure all of your husbandry techniques meet your frogs' requirements before administering medication.

Bacterial Infections

Stressed frogs may become victims of bacterial infections, such as pseudomonas infections, that result in sores and other problems. If your frog has any sores, have a veterinarian culture smears from the sores and test them for antibiotic sensitivity. Most frogs can absorb water-soluble antibiotics through their skin, so you can treat large numbers of frogs by spraying them with an appropriately diluted antibiotic solution once or twice daily, as needed. Take care not to inhale any fumes while administering the antibiotics. In serious cases, experts recommend injecting antibiotics rather than spraying them.

Red Leg

Red leg is a general term for a disease caused by *Aeromonas*. Unsanitary conditions, prolonged exposure to cold conditions, overcrowding, and other stress-inducing factors contribute to the disease. Symptoms include listlessness, bloating, lack of appetite, and a reddish appearance to the underside of the thighs and belly, caused by enlarged and broken capillaries and subcutaneous bleeding. Frogs that have contracted red leg require immediate treatment with tetracycline, administered orally at 50 mg/kg twice a day. Experts also recommend additional injectable antibiotics.

Water Edema

If a tree frog looks bloated with water, particularly in its limbs, it is likely suffering from kidney disease. Although this condition is not usually curable, it can be prevented by using proper husbandry techniques. Keep your frog's water clean at all times so that it does not reabsorb wastes (such as urine) from its water container. Other diseases, overly rich diets, and excessive supplementation can all contribute to kidney problems.

Some Indonesian White's tree frogs tend to develop large supratympanic ridges. If overfed, their ridges can get so thick as to completely cover the eyes. In time, these frogs can become partially blind.

Toxing Out

Frogs absorb water substances from their environment, particularly through the ventral area (belly skin). The absorption of harmful substances, such as ammonia, urates, and toxins, may cause convulsions, hind leg extensions, bloating, and eye clouding. You can avoid these problems by keeping your frog's environment clean and well maintained. To treat frogs suffering from these symptoms, soak them in low levels of clean water for several hours.

Drying Out

Escaped tree frogs are often found dehydrated and on the verge of death. To hydrate them, first gently remove any dust or hair that might be covering their skin with a moist cotton swab. Then place the frog in a pan of shallow water, no more than half the height of the frog at rest, inside a secure enclosure. Dehydrated frogs are often too weak to climb out of deep water and will drown. Check every six hours. Frogs will usually rehydrate in less than 24 hours. Be sure the frog's nostrils remain above water.

When necessary, use an inverted plastic spoon to open the mouth of larger tree frogs.

Here, a veterinarian administers liquid metronidazole orally with a syringe to a white-lipped tree frog.

If you need to open the mouth of a small frog, use a plastic wedge cut from a deli cup.

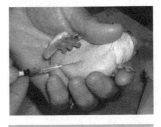

A subcutaneous enrofloxacin injection into a White's tree frog.

RESOURCES

Cogger. M.G. 1975. Reptiles and *Amphibians of Australia*. Ralph Curtis Books, 84-91.

de Vosjoli, P., and R. Mailloux. 1987. Methods and Problems of the Large Scale Propagation of Tropical Frogs. In proceedings of the Eleventh International Symposium on Captive Propagation and Husbandry, 25-34.

Duellman, W.E. 1970. *The Hylid Frogs of Middle America*. Museum of Natural History, University of Kansas.

Duellman, W.E., and L. Truebb. 1986. *Biology of the Amphibians*. McGraw Hill.

Fenolio, D. and MA. Ready. 1994. Phyllomedusine Frogs of Latin America, in the Wild and in Captivity. *The Vivarium*. 5:26-29.

Frost, D. (ed), 1985. *Amphibian Species of the World*. Lawrence, Kansas: Assoc. Sysi. Coll.

McClain, J.M., R. A. Odum, and T.C. Shely. 1983. Hormonally Induced Breeding and Rearing of White's Tree Frogs (*Litoria caerniea*). In proceedings of the Seventh Annual Reptile Symposium on Captive Propagation and Husbandry, 34-39.

Savage, J.M. and J.R. Villa. 1988. *Herpetofauna of Costa Rica*. Society for the Study of Amphibians and Reptiles.

Wright K. 1996. Amphibian Husbandry and Medicine. In *Reptile Medicine and Surgery*. W.B. Saunders Company.

ADDITIONAL INFORMATION

For more information on frogs or herpetoculture, contact one of the following:

The American Federation of Herpetoculturists (AFH) offers its members a bimonthly, full-color journal dedicated to the dissemination of information on reptiles and amphibians. Write to: PO Box 300067, Escondido, CA 92030.

The International Hylid Society, 2607 Thomas Rd., Valparaiso, IN 46383.

INDEX

ABOUT THE AUTHORS

Philippe de Vosjoli is a highly acclaimed author of the best-selling reptile-care books, The Herpetocultural Library Series. His work in the field of herpetoculture has been recognized nationally and internationally for establishing high standards for amphibian and reptile care. His books, articles, and other writings have been praised and recommended by numerous herpetological societies, veterinarians, and other experts in the field. Philippe de Vosjoli was also the cofounder and president of The American Federation of Herpetoculturists, and was given the Josef Laszlo Memorial Award in 1995 for excellence in herpetoculture and his contribution to the advancement of the field.

Robert Mailloux is a recognized pioneer in the herpetoculture of many species of amphibians and reptiles. With Philippe de Vosjoli, he has co-authored several articles and books, including *The Bearded Dragon Manual*. He owns Sandfire Dragon Ranch, a research and breeding facility in Southern California.

Drew Ready and his brother, Michael Ready (who provided many photographs for this book), have a long-standing interest in herpetoculture and photography. It is their desire to share cutting-edge information and husbandry techniques that facilitate the long-term care and breeding of amphibians in captivity. Michael Ready's photographs can be seen at http://www.michaelready.com.

CPSIA information can be obtained
at www.ICGtesting.com
Printed in the USA
LVHW06s2100210318
570658LV00007B/85/P